The Sketchbook Tool
 for
INCREASED FOCUS and CREATIVE INSIGHT

©2016 by Attentive Drawing, Inc.
All rights reserved.

Published by Attentive Drawing, Inc.

No part of this book may be reproduced without prior written permission by the publisher.

Attentive Drawing books may be purchased for educational, business, or therapeutic use through our Group Purchase Plan
group.purchase@attentive-drawing.com

ISBN-13: 978-0-6926-9571-5
ISBN-10: 0-6926-9571-0

Original artwork by Michael Shields

ATTENTIVE DRAWING is a quick and easy brain management technique that can be done anywhere.

It is a movement meditation that you do by repeatedly following along the lines of a design with pen or pencil.

There are many types of designs, each has its own feel and challenges.

Use Attentive Drawing to:

- Cleanse your "mental palette" between tasks
- Open a path for ideas and solutions from your creative unconscious
- Serve as a meditation / focus improvement tool
- Break out of a mental block
- Take a vacation from the digital world
- Get rid of stress. Have some fun!

This sketchbook is a tool for practicing Attentive Drawing. As you use it, the book also becomes a record of the ideas and insights that emerge from your creative unconscious.

Explore the different designs of Attentive Drawing in a variety of situations like work, home or a coffee shop. Try it with some of the purposes listed above in mind.

Everybody uses it in their own way.

Discover how it works for you!

Attentive Drawing quickly becomes personal to each user. We would love to see how you use it!

Share your pictures and stories and see those of other users on Instagram at

@attentivedrawing

You can learn more about the technique along with tips on how to get the most from it by visiting

attentive-drawing.com

Your feedback will help shape future designs and books.

There is no right way or wrong way to do Attentive Drawing.

Everybody uses it differently. Some people start out being very precise in how they follow the design. Others are loose and flowing.

Try different approaches. Like any practice it may take some time to find the ways you like to use it

If you need to change your mindset, being very accurate with an intricate design may be just what you need.

If you need to loosen up and take some risks, try a relaxed approach with how you interact with a flowing design.

An example of a looser approach to a medium intricacy design:

The design has been followed several times, back and forth, possibly over different sessions.

Yours may look like this, it may not. The key is to get started, try different ways and be open to whatever comes to you.

On the next page is that same design, called *Bird Dance*, for you to try.

Start at one end (found in the middle) and follow to the other end - then reverse course.

As you repeat this process don't be surprised if you go off the path without realizing it! It can take more attention than you expect.

As the title suggests, following this design can have a "dance' like feel to it.

The designs are printed in a light gray so that more of your attention is required to follow along the line.

All designs will be on one side of a page. The other side may have comments about the design or quotations but they will be mainly blank for you to jot notes or make sketches of ideas and solutions that emerge while you follow the design.

In this way, the books become treasured creative journals that you can keep as a personal resource.

NOTES/SKETCHES:

Bird Dance

This design, *Mazy Way*, is another end to end design where you start at one end of the design line, continue to the other end, then return back along the path to where you began.

It was inspired by another type of movement meditation - walking along a labyrinth.

NOTES/SKETCHES:

Some designs have no beginning and no end, you can start anywhere and stop anywhere.

This one, *Infinity Lotus*, is fun and flowing but becomes surprisingly more challenging with each pass through the design.

NOTES/SKETCHES:

Note the difference in feel between this design, *Lotus*, and the previous one, *Lotus Infinity*. It is a great introduction into perceiving the different qualities of the designs.

NOTES/SKETCHES:

Lotus

Be sure to experiment! Pen has a very different feel than pencil. Try both! Have fun with colored pencils and pens.

Turn the book around. Some positions might be helpful for certain designs.

Play! Draw patterns in the spaces of finished designs. Color them in!

Make Attentive Drawing your own!

NOTES/SKETCHES:

Decision Circle can help you break out of a pattern of thinking or decision making.

As you follow the design, note areas that are getting neglected by your path choices. Finding ways to give them equal coverage forces you out of the path you are most comfortable taking.

NOTES/SKETCHES:

Decision Circle

NOTES/SKETCHES:

It's not about having any particular experience. The practice is about opening to whatever presents itself.

- Joel Goldsmith

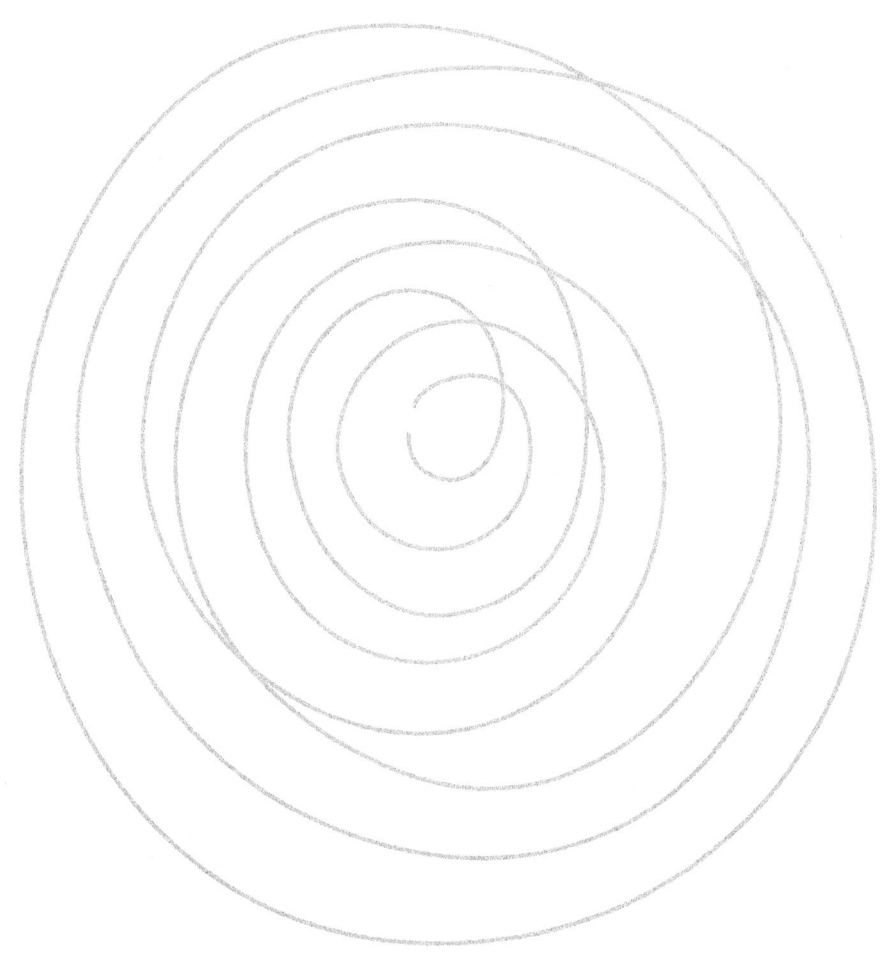

Organic Spiral

Now the designs begin to repeat so that you can try them each several times to learn how they work for you. There are seven different designs in this book.

You may prefer following some over others but keep trying them all. These designs can fill different needs at different times.

NOTES/SKETCHES:

NOTES/SKETCHES:

NOTES/SKETCHES:

infinity Lotus

NOTES/SKETCHES:

Lotus

NOTES/SKETCHES:

NOTES/SKETCHES:

Decision Circle

NOTES/SKETCHES:

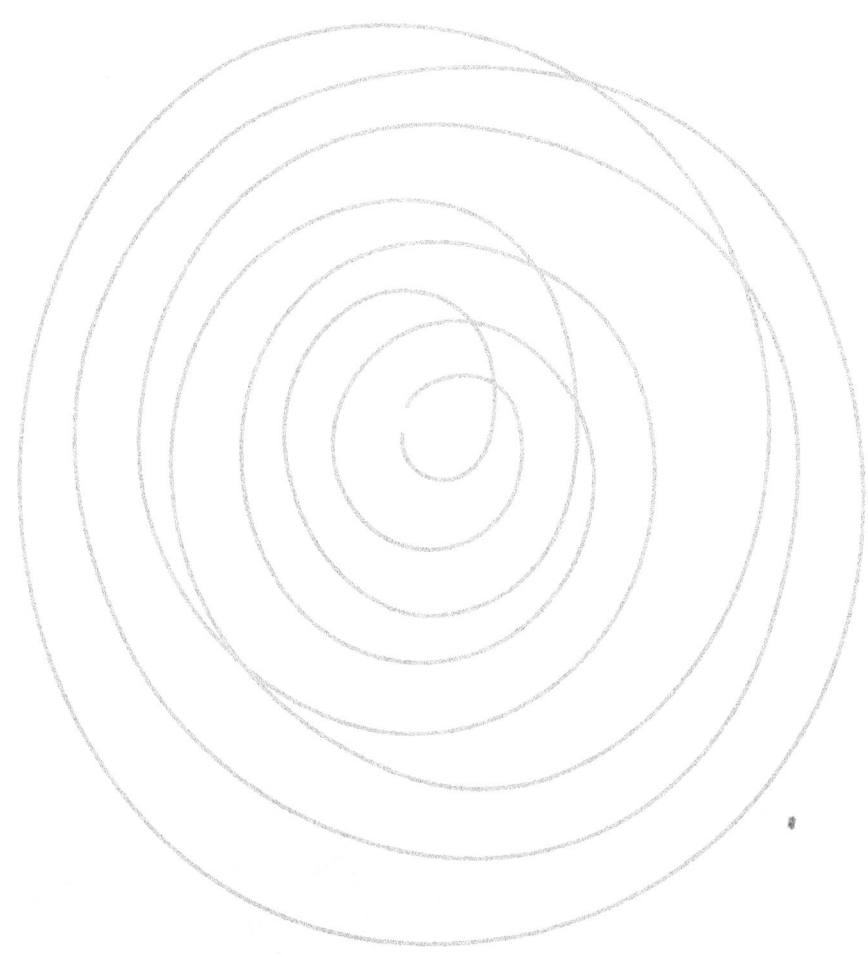

Organic Spiral

NOTES/SKETCHES:

Through meditation and by giving full attention to one thing at a time, we can learn to direct attention where we choose.

- Eknath Easwaran

Bird Dance

NOTES/SKETCHES:

Mazy Way

NOTES/SKETCHES:

Infinity Lotus

NOTES/SKETCHES:

Lotus

NOTES/SKETCHES:

Piping

NOTES/SKETCHES:

Decision Circle

NOTES/SKETCHES:

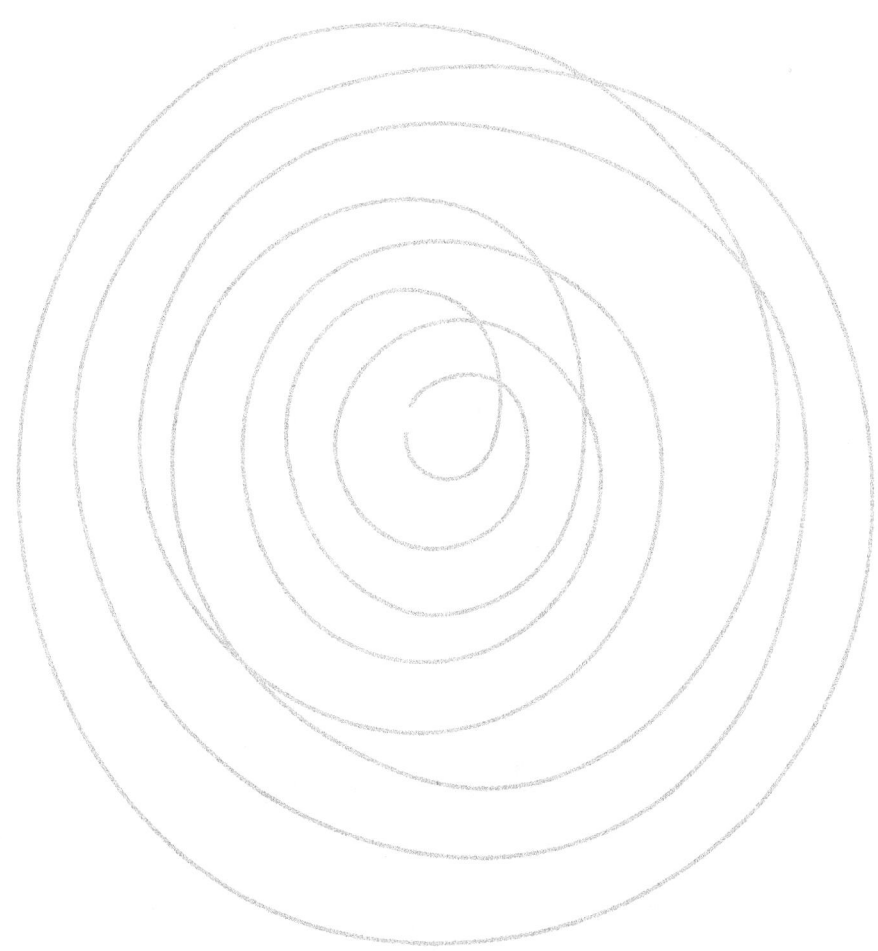

NOTES/SKETCHES:

Take the time to come home to yourself every day.

- Robin Casarjean

Bird Dance

NOTES/SKETCHES:

NOTES/SKETCHES:

NOTES/SKETCHES:

Lotus

NOTES/SKETCHES:

NOTES/SKETCHES:

Decision Circle

NOTES/SKETCHES:

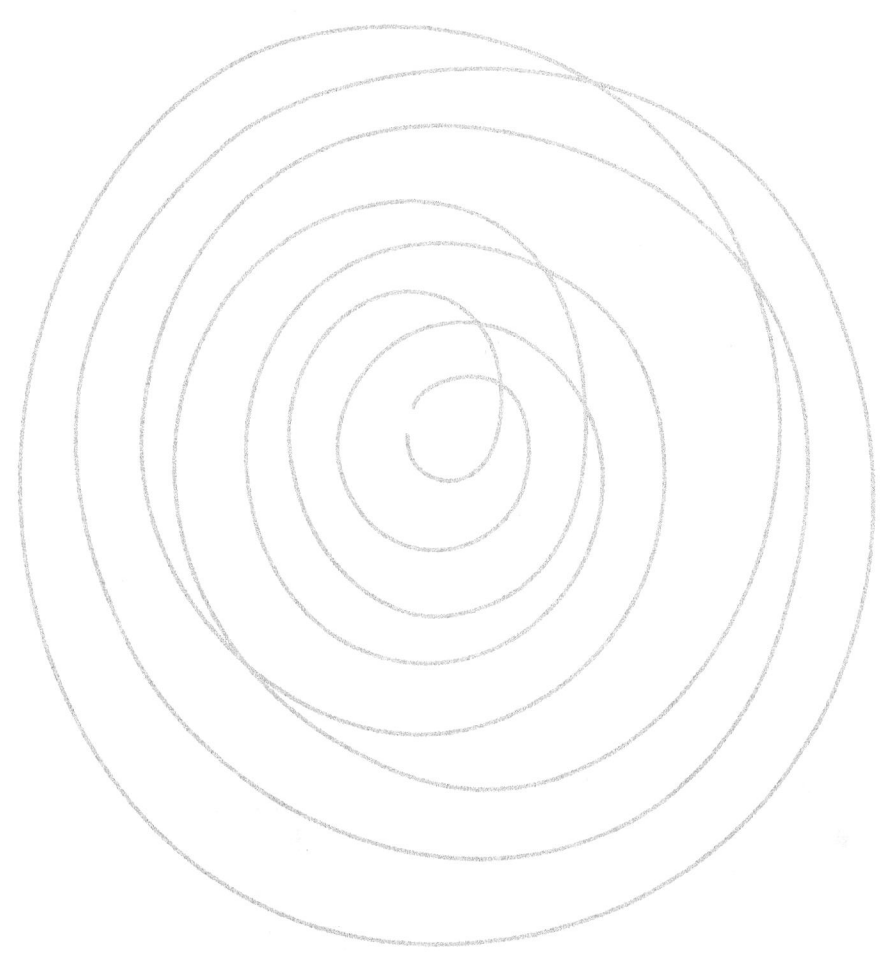

Organic Spiral

NOTES/SKETCHES:

Bird Dance

NOTES/SKETCHES:

Mazy Way

NOTES/SKETCHES:

Infinity Lotus

NOTES/SKETCHES:

Lotus

NOTES/SKETCHES:

NOTES/SKETCHES:

Decision Circle

NOTES/SKETCHES:

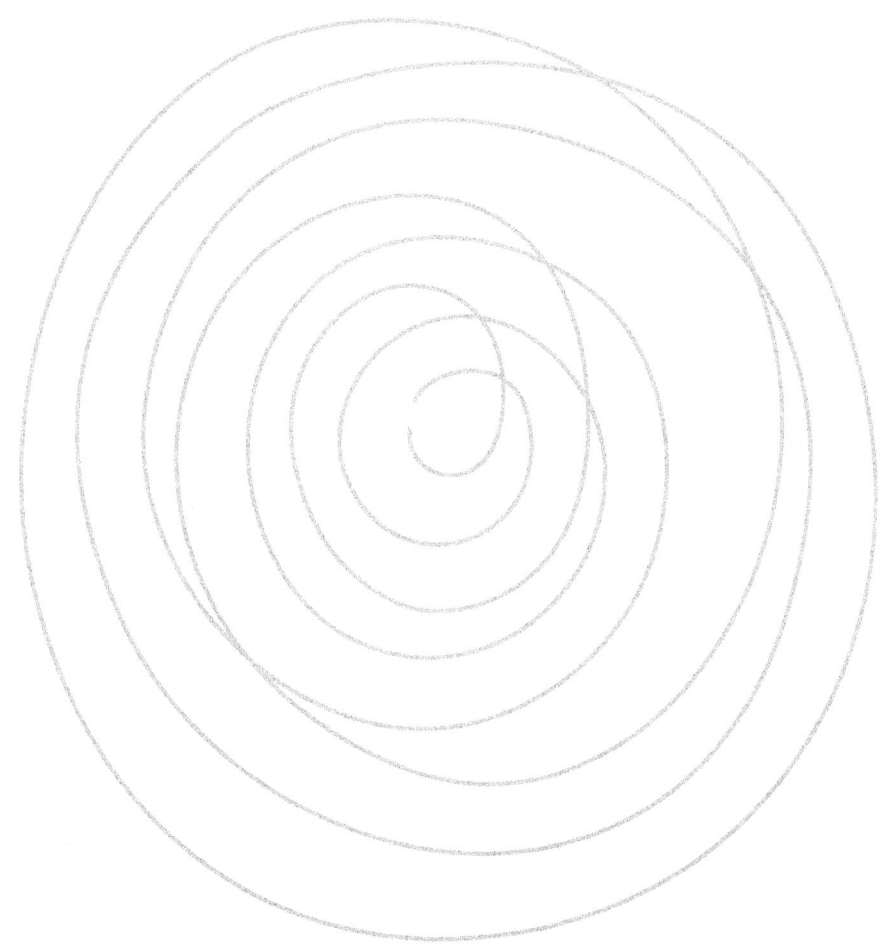

Organic Spiral

NOTES/SKETCHES:

Bird Dance

NOTES/SKETCHES:

NOTES/SKETCHES:

Infinity Lotus

NOTES/SKETCHES:

Lotus

NOTES/SKETCHES:

NOTES/SKETCHES:

Decision Circle

NOTES/SKETCHES:

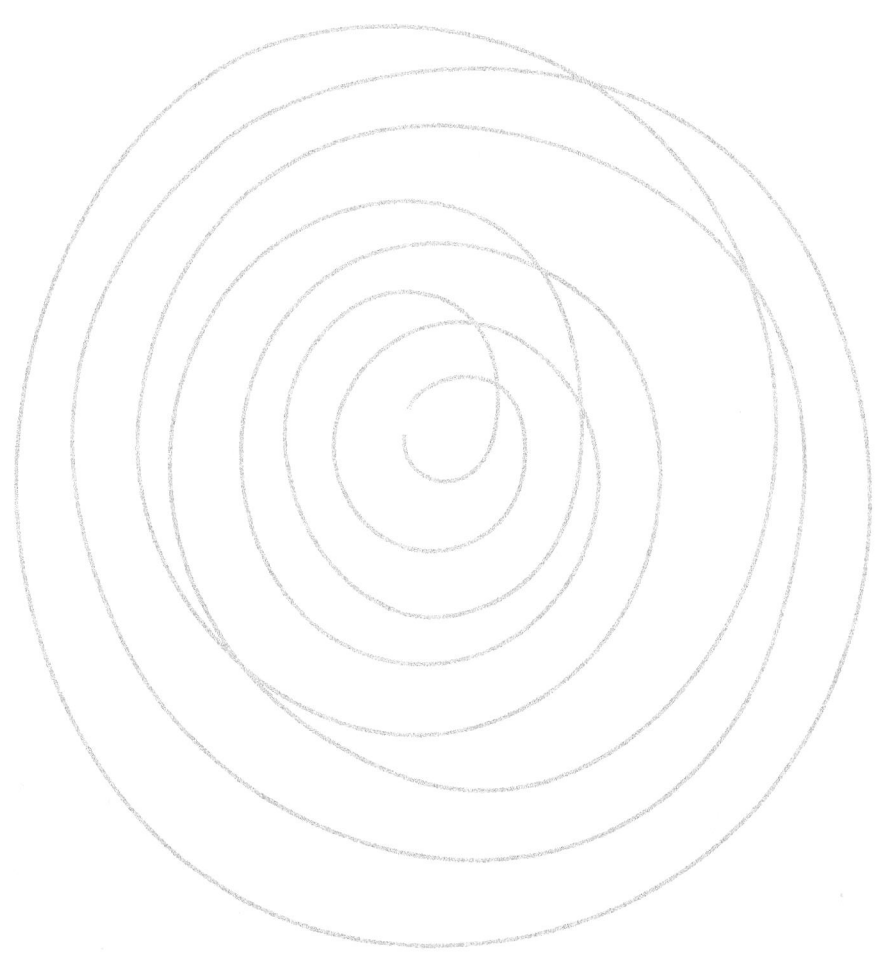

Organic Spiral

NOTES/SKETCHES:

Bird Dance

NOTES/SKETCHES:

NOTES/SKETCHES:

Infinity Lotus

NOTES/SKETCHES:

NOTES/SKETCHES:

Piping

NOTES/SKETCHES:

Decision Circle

NOTES/SKETCHES:

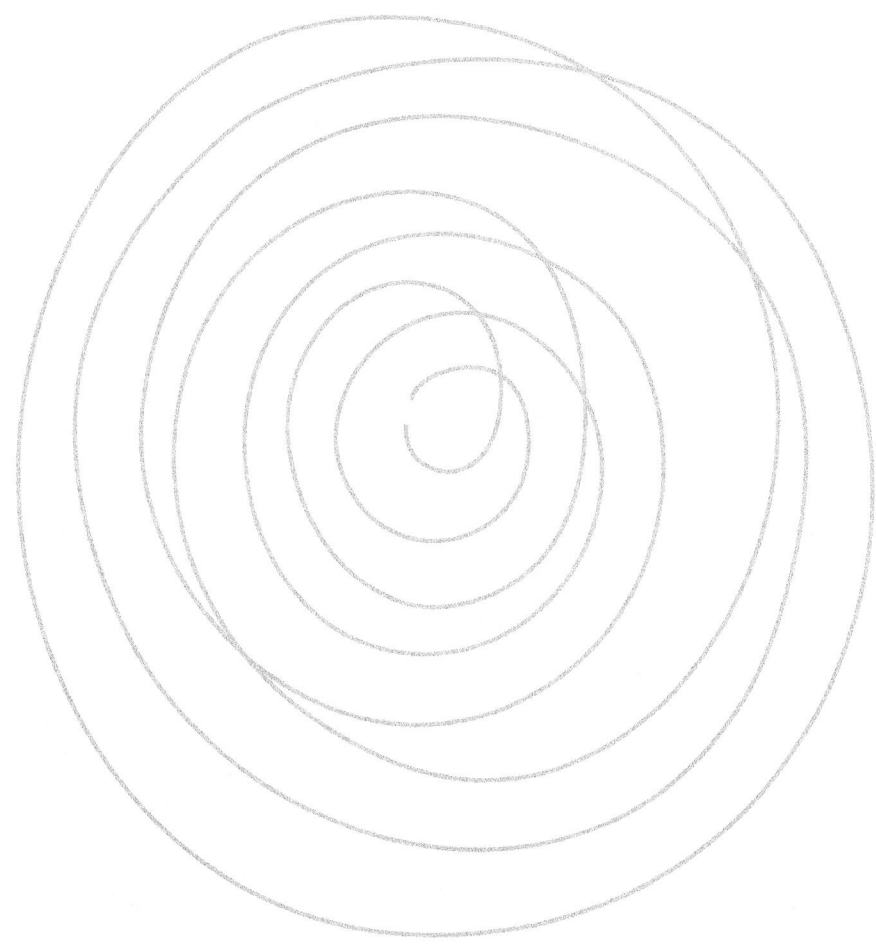

Organic Spiral

www.ingramcontent.com/pod-product-compliance
Lightning Source LLC
Chambersburg PA
CBHW071724040426
42446CB00011B/2210